All-Occasion CARDS With Cricut™

Annie's Attic®

All-Occasion Cards With Cricut™

EDITOR Tanya Fox
CREATIVE DIRECTOR Brad Snow
PUBLISHING SERVICES DIRECTOR Brenda Gallmeyer
ASSOCIATE EDITOR Brooke Smith
ASSISTANT ART DIRECTOR Nick Pierce
COPY SUPERVISOR Deborah Morgan
COPY EDITORS Mary O'Donnell, Sam Schneider
TECHNICAL EDITOR Corene Painter
PHOTOGRAPHY SUPERVISOR Tammy Christian
PHOTOGRAPHY Matt Bowen, Matthew Owen
PHOTO STYLISTS Tammy Liechty, Tammy Steiner
PRODUCTION ARTIST SUPERVISOR Erin Augsbuger
GRAPHIC ARTIST Nicole Gage
PRODUCTION ASSISTANTS Marj Morgan, Judy Neuenschwander

Printed in the United States of America
First Printing: 2011
ISBN: 978-1-59635-385-5
1 2 3 4 5 6 7 8 9 10 11 12

Contents

Birthday Cards

Get Well Cards

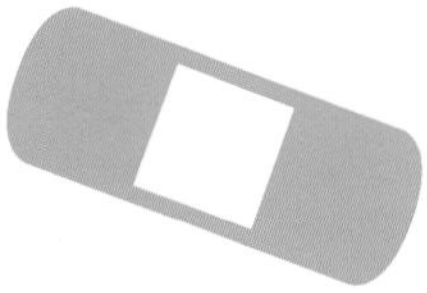

Thank You Cards

Sympathy Cards

Thninking of You Cards

Congratulations Cards

Shop Til You Drop

Design by **Kimber McGray**

Using Lyrical Letters cartridge and Passion Fruit Dot paper, cut 3-inch card base by selecting Capital feature; press "<shift>" and "<HappyBday>." Fold at marks to create matchbook card base.

Using Paisley cartridge and Meatballs paper, cut a 2½-inch purse by pressing "<Purse2>." Cut a 2½-inch purse top from olive green cardstock by pressing "<shift>" and "<Purse2>." Cut a 2½-inch purse handle from Buttercup Dot paper by selecting Layer 1 feature; press "<Purse2>." Cut a 2½-inch purse button from white cardstock by selecting Layer 1 feature; press "<shift>" and "<Purse2>."

Cut a 2½-inch "Shop til you drop" from white cardstock by selecting Word feature; press "<Purse2>."

Layer and adhere purse pieces together as shown. Attach to card front using foam tape. Attach a gem to purse button. Wrap ribbon around bottom flap of card front. Tie bow and trim ends.

Adhere sentiment inside top flap of card. Embellish with gems. If desired, secure gift card inside card using repositionable tape. ●

Sources: Cricut Expression machine and cartridges from Provo Craft; cardstock from Core'dinations; Double Dot printed papers from Bo-Bunny Press; Meatballs printed paper from Jillibean Soup; self-adhesive gems from Queen & Co.; ribbon from Creative Impressions Inc.

Materials

- Cricut Expression machine
- Cartridges: Lyrical Letters (#29-0708), Paisley (#29-1591)
- Cardstock: olive green, white
- Printed papers: Double Dot Passion Fruit Dot, Double Dot Buttercup Dot, Pasta Fagioli Meatballs
- Various sizes of olive green self-adhesive gems
- 15 inches ½-inch-wide white silk ribbon
- Adhesive foam tape
- Repositionable tape (optional)
- Paper adhesive

Enjoy

Design by **Melissa Phillips**

Project note: *Ink edges of all cut pieces light brown.*

Using Graphically Speaking cartridge and J'adore Glittered paper, cut a 6-inch file folder card base by selecting Icon feature; press "<Image32>." Fold in half to create a bottom-folded card.

Cut a 4-inch half flower from Rose Bouquet paper by selecting Phrase feature; press "<shift>" and "<Image45>."

Cut a 2-inch "enjoy" from brown/black paper by selecting Type feature; press "<Image30>."

Cut a 6⅛ x ¾-inch piece from Ebony paper. Adhere to card front as shown; trim edges to align edges with card front edges. Adhere decorative lace along top edge of Ebony strip. Adhere half flower and "enjoy" to card front as shown.

Thread button with white twine; tie knot on back, trim ends. Adhere to half flower. Attach gem to "j" in "enjoy."

Cut doily in half; adhere inside card, overlapping notch in card front.

Tie a knot in middle of seam binding. Tie a knot in middle of text print ribbon. Staple knotted ribbons to file folder as shown. ●

Sources: Cricut Expression machine and cartridge from Provo Craft; J'adore Glittered printed paper from My Mind's Eye; Rose Bouquet printed paper from Echo Park Paper Co.; Ebony printed paper from Heart & Home Collectables Inc./Melissa Frances; Trim Staples ribbon from Graphic 45.

Materials

- Cricut Expression machine
- Cartridge: Graphically Speaking (#29-0590)
- Printed papers: Lost & Found Madison Avenue Girlfriends J'adore Glittered, Be Mine Rose Bouquet, 5th Avenue Ebony, brown/black
- 3¾-inch white paper doily
- Light brown ink pad
- Large gray self-adhesive gem
- Large cream button
- White twine
- Ribbon: 6⅛ inches ⅝-inch-wide cream lace, 3 inches ½-inch-wide cream seam binding, 4 inches ⅜-inch-wide Trim Staples black/white text print
- Stapler
- Paper adhesive

Ice Cream Cone Card

Design by **Melissa Phillips**

Project note: *Ink edges of all cut pieces.*

Using Sweet Treats cartridge and cream cardstock, cut a 6-inch ice cream cone card base by selecting Cards feature; press "<Icecrm6>."

Cut a 6-inch bottom layer of ice cream from cream/pink floral paper by selecting Layers feature; press "<Icecrm6>."

Cut a 6-inch middle layer for ice cream from Library Ledger paper by selecting Layers feature; press "<shift>" and "<Icecrm6>." Repeat cut using Pink Dot paper.

Cut a 6-inch heart from Pink Dot paper by selecting Layers feature; press "<shift>" and "<Cupcake5>."

Adhere pompom trim to bottom edge of bottom ice cream layer. Adhere to card front as shown.

Wrap seam binding around card front over bottom layer of ice cream. Tie bow on right edge; trim ends. Adhere remaining ice cream layers and heart to card front as shown.

Thread button with thread; tie knot on back, trim ends. Layer and adhere paper flower and button to top of ice cream as shown.

Embellish heart with pearl. ●

Sources: Cricut Expression machine and cartridge from Provo Craft; Library Ledger printed paper from Papertrey Ink; Pink Dot printed paper from Making Memories.

Materials

- Cricut Expression machine
- Cartridge: Sweet Treats (#29-1557)
- Cream cardstock
- Printed papers: brown/cream Library Ledger, Je t'Adore Pink Dot, cream/pink floral
- Light brown ink pad
- Small brown self-adhesive pearl
- Cream paper flower
- Cream button
- 4 inches white pompom trim
- 14 inches ½-inch-wide pink seam binding
- Pink thread
- Paper adhesive

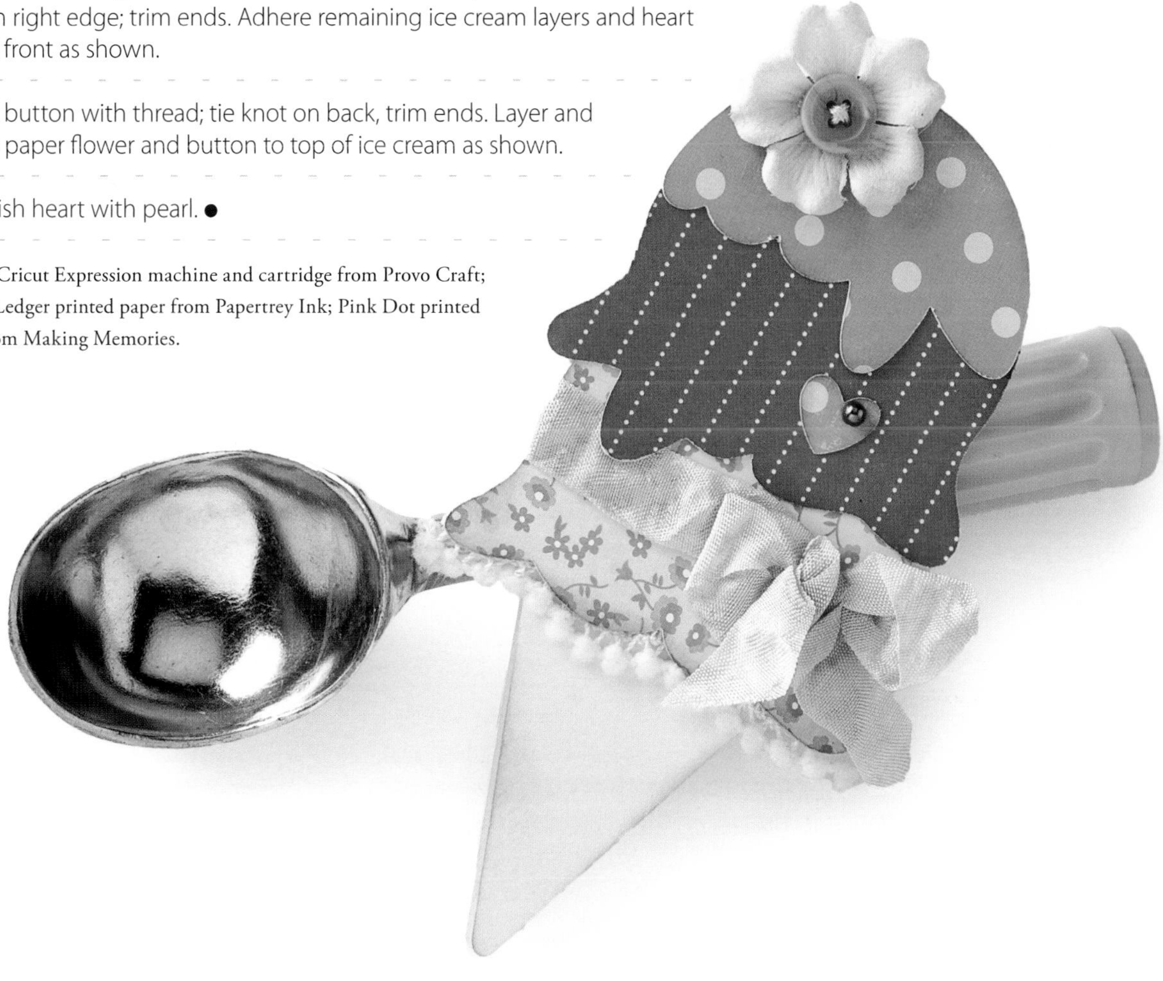

Happy Birthday

Design by **Summer Fullerton**

Using Sweet Treats cartridge and brown cardstock, cut a 5-inch "happy birthday" by selecting Layers feature; press "<Cake4>."

Cut a 2½-inch party hat base from yellow cardstock by pressing "<Hat2>."

Cut a 2½-inch second layer of party hat from green cardstock by pressing "<shift>" and "<Hat2>."

Cut a 2½-inch top layer of party hat from Unwrapped Presents paper by selecting Layers feature; press "<Hat2>."

Cut a 2½-inch top of party hat from white cardstock by selecting Layers feature; press "<shift>" and "<Hat2>."

Layer and adhere party hat pieces together as shown. Embellish with gem.

Form a 4 x 6-inch side-folded card from kraft cardstock.

Cut a 3⅝ x 5⅝-inch piece from Silly Owls paper; round top corners. Cut a 3⅝ x 1⅝-inch piece from Totally Fun Tunes paper. Adhere to Silly Owls panel, aligning bottom edges.

Wrap ribbon around layered panel as shown. Tie bow; trim ends. Adhere to card front. Adhere sentiment to card front as shown. Referring to photo, attach party hat to card front using foam tape. ●

Sources: Cricut Expression machine and cartridge from Provo Craft; cardstock from Bazzill Basics Paper Inc.; printed papers from Jillibean Soup.

Materials

- Cricut Expression machine
- Cartridge: Sweet Treats (#29-1557)
- Cardstock: green, kraft, white, yellow, brown
- Spotted Owl Soup printed papers: Unwrapped Presents, Silly Owls, Totally Fun Tunes
- 16½ inches ⅝-inch-wide light green ribbon
- Silver self-adhesive gem
- Corner rounder
- Adhesive foam tape
- Paper adhesive

Happy Day

Design by **Kandis Smith**

Using Wedding Solutions cartridge and aqua cardstock, cut a 2¼-inch tag by pressing "<shift>" and "<bookplate>."

Using Walk in My Garden cartridge and yellow cardstock, cut a 1¼-inch "happy" by pressing "<happy>."

Using Plantin SchoolBook cartridge and pink cardstock, cut a 1¾-inch star by pressing "<star>."

Cut a ¾-inch "DAY" from green cardstock by pressing "<shiftlock>," "<D>," "<A>" and "<Y>."

Form a 5½ x 5½-inch top-folded card from green cardstock. Adhere a 5⅛ x 3¼-inch piece of Flour Sack paper to card front as shown.

Cut a 5⅛ x 2-inch piece from red cardstock. Using Swiss Dots embossing folder, emboss red panel. Adhere to card front as shown.

Machine-stitch around top, left and right sides of Flour Sack panel. Zigzag-stitch where Flour Sack and embossed panels meet.

Cut twill tape in half. Thread one piece of twill through hole on tag, folding one end over as shown. Pierce hole through twill; insert brad, securing twill to tag. Repeat with second piece of twill and remaining hole on tag. Attach tag to card front using foam tape. Wrap unsecured ends of twill around card front; secure inside card.

Attach star to tag using foam tape. Thread button with baker's twine; tie bow on front, trim ends. Adhere button to star.

Attach "happy" to card front as shown, using foam tape. Adhere "DAY" below "happy." ●

Sources: Cricut Expression machine, cartridges and embossing folder from Provo Craft; cardstock from Bazzill Basics Paper Inc.; printed paper from October Afternoon.

Materials

- Cricut Expression machine
- Cartridges: Plantin SchoolBook (#29-0390), Walk in My Garden (#29-0223), Wedding Solutions (#29-0544)
- Cardstock: green, red, aqua, pink, yellow
- Modern Homemaker Flour Sack printed paper
- 2 yellow brads
- Large red button
- 8 inches ⅜-inch-wide cream twill tape
- Red/white baker's twine
- Swiss Dots embossing folder (#37-1604)
- Embossing machine
- Paper piercer
- Sewing machine with white thread
- Adhesive foam tape
- Paper adhesive

Birthday Cupcake

Design by **Jennifer Buck**

Materials

- Cricut Expression machine
- Cartridge: Wild Card (#29-0591)
- Cardstock: kraft, light yellow, light blue
- Spotted Owl Soup printed papers: Dancing Hats, Unwrapped Presents
- Various sizes of red buttons
- Adhesive foam tape
- Paper adhesive

Using Wild Card cartridge and Dancing Hats paper, cut a 6-inch cupcake card base by pressing "<Cupcake>." Fold at marks to create a side-folded card with a cupcake front.

Cut a 6-inch cupcake wrapper from kraft cardstock by selecting Icon feature; press "<Cupcake>."

Cut a 6-inch cupcake top from Unwrapped Present paper by selecting Icon feature; press "<shift>" and "<Cupcake>."

Cut a 6-inch candle from light yellow cardstock by selecting Liner feature; press "<Cupcake>." Repeat cut using light blue cardstock; cut flame off light blue candle.

Layer and adhere cupcake pieces to card front as shown, using foam tape to pop-up cupcake top layer. Embellish cupcake with buttons as shown. ●

Sources: Cricut Expression machine and cartridge from Provo Craft; printed papers from Jillibean Soup.

Happy Birthday Dad

Design by **Lynn Ghahary**

Materials

- Cricut Expression machine
- Cartridges: Nifty Fifties (#20-00586), Martha Stewart Crafts Birthday Cake Art (#20-00898)
- Cardstock: red, light blue, black, white
- Printed papers: light brown grid, green, stripe
- 2 black brads
- Round Binding Edge Edger Punch
- Paper piercer
- Sewing machine with white thread
- Adhesive foam tape
- Paper adhesive

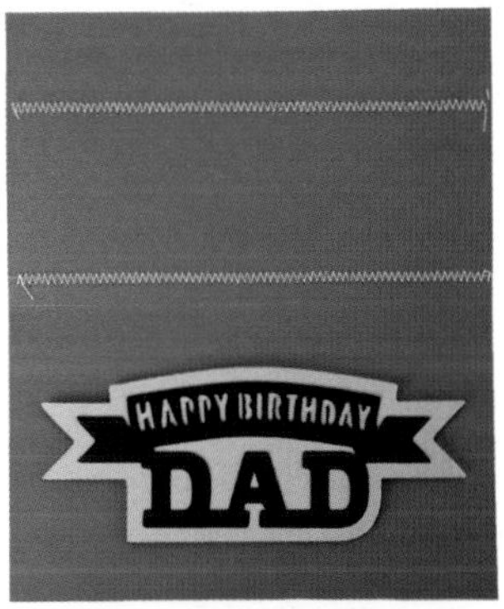

Using Nifty Fifties cartridge and black cardstock, cut a 2-inch car base by pressing "<Car1>."

Cut a 2-inch second layer for car from light blue cardstock by pressing "<shift>" and "<Car1>." Cut a 2-inch third layer for car from red cardstock by selecting Layer 1 feature; press "<Car1>."

Cut a 2-inch top layer for car from white cardstock by selecting Layer 1 feature; press "<shift>" and "<Car1>."

Using Martha Stewarts Crafts Birthday Cake Art cartridge and black cardstock, cut a 2-inch "HAPPY BIRTHDAY DAD" by selecting Phrase feature; press "<Banner3>."

Cut a 2-inch bottom layer for sentiment from light blue cardstock by selecting Phrase feature; press "<shift>" and "<Banner3>."

Layer and adhere car pieces together as shown. Pierce two holes in wheels and insert black brads.

Form a 7 x 4⅛-inch top-folded card from red cardstock.

Cut 7 x 2⅜-inch piece from light brown grid paper. Cut a 7 x 1-inch piece from green printed paper; punch one long edge using Round Binding Edge Edger Punch. Cut a 7 x ½-inch piece from stripe paper. Layer and adhere cut pieces to card front as shown.

Zigzag-stitch top and bottom edges of light brown grid piece. Attach assembled car to card front using foam tape.

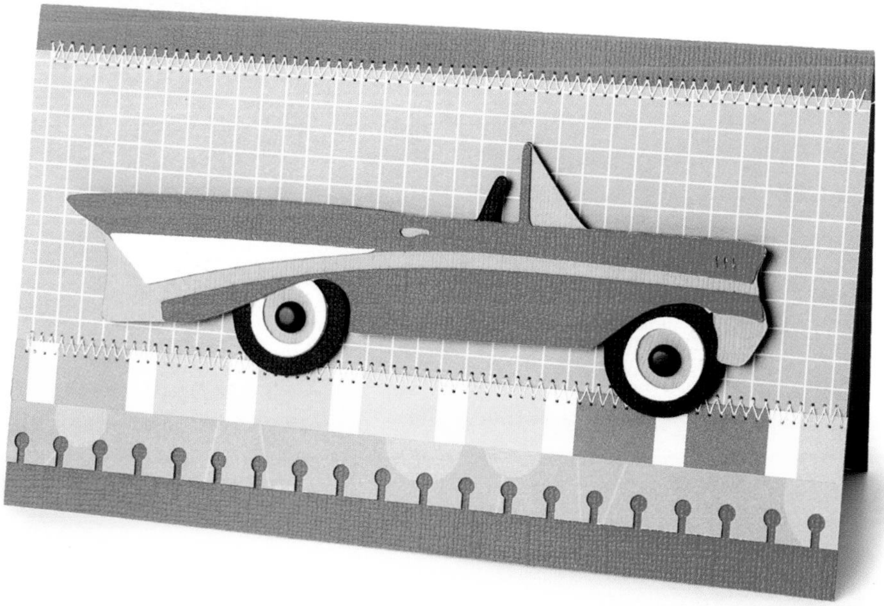

Layer and adhere sentiment pieces together. Attach inside card using foam tape. ●

Sources: Cricut Expression machine and cartridges from Provo Craft; red and light blue cardstock from Bazzill Basics Paper Inc.; white and black cardstock from American Crafts Inc.; Notebook Edge Punch from EK Success.

Happy B-day

Design by **Sherry Wright**

Using Storybook cartridge and white cardstock, cut a 6-inch card base by selecting Accent Blackout feature; press "<shift>" and "<thank you>." Repeat cut using Sunrise paper.

Using Home Décor cartridge and black cardstock, cut two 1½-inch bees by selecting Blackout feature; press "<Bee>" and "<Bee>."

Using Wild Card cartridge and cream cardstock, cut a 4½-inch circle by selecting Liner feature; press "<Pinwheel>." Ink edges of circle gray.

Cut a 1½-inch "Happy B-day" from black cardstock by selecting Phrase feature; press "<Cupcake>." Trim "B" and "day" from cut sentiment; use center piece from "d" to create hyphen.

Layer and adhere card base piece together as shown. Wrap ribbon around left side of card front, tie bow and trim ends with decorative-edge scissors.

Layer and adhere circle, sentiment and bees to card front as shown. Embellish bees with gems. ●

Sources: Cricut Expression machine and cartridges from Provo Craft; cardstock from Bazzill Basics Paper Inc.; printed paper from Cosmo Cricket; self-adhesive gems from Zva Creative.

Materials

- Cricut Expression machine
- Cartridges:
  Storybook (#29-0589),
  Home Décor (#29-0695),
  Wild Card (#29-0591)
- Cardstock: black, white, cream
- Early Bird Sunrise printed paper
- Gray ink pad
- 24 inches ¾-inch-wide yellow ribbon
- 4 yellow self-adhesive gems
- Decorative-edge scissors
- Paper adhesive

Feel Better

Design by **Kandis Smith**

Materials

- Cricut Expression machine
- Cartridges: Winter Woodland (#29-1046), Walk in My Garden (#29-0223), Plantin SchoolBook (#29-0390)
- Cardstock: aqua, red, brown, green, pink
- Quite Contrary Jack & Jill Sooo Cute Engaging Gingham printed paper
- 7 inches ¼-inch-wide teal ribbon
- Corner rounder
- Sandpaper
- Sewing machine with white thread
- Adhesive foam dots
- Paper adhesive

Using Winter Woodland cartridge and red cardstock, cut a 5-inch scalloped panel by pressing "<Snowflk2>." Using sandpaper, distress edges of scalloped panel. Cut a 5-inch square from Engaging Gingham paper by pressing "<shift>" and "<Snowflk2>."

Using Walk in My Garden cartridge and brown cardstock, cut a 1¼-inch flowerpot by pressing "<flwrpt>." Cut 1¼-inch top rim of flowerpot from brown cardstock by pressing "<shift>" and "<flwrpt>." Distress edges of both flowerpot pieces using sandpaper.

Cut 3-inch tulips from green cardstock by pressing "<tulip>." Cut 3-inch tulip flowers from pink cardstock by pressing "<shift>" and "<tulip>."

Using Plantin SchoolBook cartridge and pink cardstock, cut a ¾-inch "feel better" by pressing "<f>," "<e>," "<e>," "<l>," "<b>," "<e>," "<t>," "<t>," "<e>" and "<r>."

Form a 5½ x 5½-inch top-folded card from aqua cardstock. Use corner rounder to round all four corners of card. Distress edges of card front with sandpaper.

Adhere Engaging Gingham square to scalloped panel. Machine-stitch along edge of square. Attach to card front using foam dots.

Adhere pink tulip flowers to green tulips. Attach to card front using foam dots as shown.

Attach flowerpot to card front as shown, using foam dots. In the same manner, attach flowerpot rim to flowerpot.

Tie a bow with ribbon; trim ends. Adhere to flowerpot rim.

Adhere "feel better" to card front as shown. ●

Sources: Cricut Expression machine and cartridges from Provo Craft; cardstock from Core'dinations; printed paper from My Mind's Eye.

Hang In There

Design by **Lynn Ghahary**

Using Create A Critter cartridge and green cardstock, cut a 3½-inch vine by selecting Accessory feature; press "<shift>" and "<Monkey>." Repeat cut.

Cut a 3½-inch bottom layer of monkey from Sassy Cat paper by pressing "<Monkey>."

Cut a 3½-inch middle layer of monkey from light brown cardstock by selecting Layer 1 feature; press "<Monkey>."

Cut a 3½-inch top layer of monkey from brown cardstock by selecting Layer 2 feature; press "<Monkey>."

Using Wild Card cartridge and green cardstock, cut a 7-inch "Hang in there" by selecting Phrase feature; press "<shift>" and "<Tweety>."

Form a 4¼ x 5½-inch side-folded card from Sassy Cat paper as shown.

Cut a 3¼ x 5½-inch piece from Top Dog paper. Adhere a 3 x 3⅞-inch piece of white cardstock to Top Dog piece as shown. Trim left end of ribbon at an angle. Wrap ribbon around layered panel covering bottom edge of white panel. Allow left end of ribbon to extend past edge of panel. Adhere to card front.

Using foam dots, attach a vine to the other vine. ***Note:*** *Trim dots down as needed.* Adhere layered vines to card front as shown.

Layer and adhere monkey pieces together. Attach to card front using foam dots; tuck monkey's arm under vine.

Attach brad to card front as shown using foam dots.

Cut a 3 x 3⅞-inch piece from white cardstock. Adhere "Hang in there" sentiment to white panel. Adhere inside card. ●

Sources: Cricut Expression machine and cartridges from Provo Craft; cardstock from Core'dinations; printed papers and ribbon from Pebbles Inc.; brad from My Mind's Eye.

Materials

- Cricut Expression machine
- Cartridges: Create A Critter (#20-00099), Wild Card (#29-0591)
- Cardstock: white, light brown, brown, green
- Cats & Dogs printed papers: Sassy Cat, Top Dog
- Lush green decorative brad
- 2 googly eyes
- 8 inches ⅝-inch-wide orange/white stitched ribbon
- Adhesive foam dots
- Paper adhesive

Milk It

Design by **Jennifer Buck**

Materials

- Cricut Expression machine
- Cartridge: "Just Because" Cards (#20-00097)
- Cardstock: kraft, black, white
- Blossom Soup Anejo Cheese printed paper
- Brown distress dye ink pad
- 23 inches ½-inch-wide black/white gingham ribbon
- Adhesive foam dots
- Paper adhesive

Using "Just Because" Cards cartridge and kraft cardstock, cut a 5½-inch scalloped-edge card base by pressing "<Apple>."

Cut a 5½-inch scalloped edge from black cardstock by pressing "<shift>" and "<Apple>."

Cut a 7-inch milk jug from black cardstock by selecting Layer 1 feature; press "<Milk>."

Cut a 7-inch milk jug from white cardstock by selecting Layer 1 feature; press "<shift>" and "<Milk>."

Cut a 2¾-inch "feeling sick? Milk IT" from black cardstock by selecting Word feature; press "<Milk>."

Adhere black scalloped edge to scalloped edge of card front.

Adhere white milk jug to black milk jug.

Cut a 3½ x 1¾-inch piece from black cardstock and a 3½ x 1½-inch piece from Anejo Cheese paper. Layer and adhere to card front as shown.

Using foam dots, attach milk jug to card front as shown. Wrap ribbon around left side of card front; tie bow, trim ends.

Adhere sentiment inside card. ***Note:*** *Remove "?" before adhering sentiment inside card, if desired.* ●

Sources: Cricut Expression machine and cartridge from Provo Craft; printed paper from Jillibean Soup.

To Perk You Up

Design by **Kelly Goree**

Using Plantin SchoolBook cartridge and Stripe Passion Fruit paper, cut a 1-inch scallop by pressing "<scallop>."

Using Beyond Birthdays cartridge and kraft cardstock, cut a 2-inch coffee cup by pressing "<mug>."

Cut a 3-inch steam swirl from Perky Paper by pressing "<shift>" and "<mug>."

Using Simply Sweet cartridge and Stripe Passion Fruit paper, cut a 1-inch heart by pressing "<shift>" and "<flower>."

Cut a 2-inch "get well soon" by pressing "<getwell>."

Form a 4¼ x 5½-inch side-folded card from white cardstock. Adhere a 4¼ x 5½-inch piece of hot pink cardstock to card front.

Cut a 4 x 5¼-inch piece from Journal Chocolate paper and a 4 x 1¼-inch piece from Perky Paper. Using fine-tip pen, draw two dotted lines along bottom edge of Perky Paper piece. Trim scalloped piece to 4 inches in length. Layer and adhere pieces to card front as shown.

Adhere coffee cup, steam and sentiment to card front as shown.

Using fine-tip pen, draw a border around heart. Attach to coffee cup using foam dots. ●

Sources: Cricut Expression machine and cartridges from Provo Craft; cardstock from Bazzill Basics Paper Inc.; printed papers from Bo-Bunny Press.

Materials

- Cricut Expression machine
- Cartridges: Plantin SchoolBook (#29-0390), Beyond Birthdays (#29-0024), Simply Sweet (#29-0704)
- Cardstock: kraft, white, hot pink
- Printed papers: Vicki B. Perky Paper, Stripe Passion Fruit, Journal Chocolate
- Brown fine-tip pen
- Adhesive foam dots
- Paper adhesive

Just for You

Design by **Lynn Ghahary**

Materials

- Cricut Expression machine
- Cartridges: Freshly Picked (#20-00313), Wild Card (#29-0591)
- Cardstock: white, lavender, purple, light brown, brown, light green, green
- Sugar Plum Plum Passion printed paper
- White gel pen
- 5 purple self-adhesive gems
- Purple button
- 23 inches ⅜-inch-wide green/white dot ribbon
- White thread
- Scallop Edge Border Punch
- Adhesive foam dots
- Paper adhesive

Using Freshly Picked cartridge and brown cardstock, cut a 3-inch flowerpot by pressing "<Flower4>."

Cut a 3-inch top rim of flowerpot from light brown cardstock by pressing "<shift>" and "<Flower4>." **Note:** *Flowers from this cut will not be used.*

Cut a 3-inch leaf base from green cardstock by selecting Layers feature; press "<Flower4>."

Cut a 3-inch top layer of leaves from light green cardstock by selecting Layers feature; press "<shift>" and "<Flowers4>."

Cut a 3-inch flower base from purple cardstock by selecting Layers 2 feature; press "<Flowers4>."

Cut a 3-inch top layer of flowers from lavender cardstock by pressing "<shift>" and "<Flower4>." **Note:** *Rim of flowerpot from this cut will not be used.*

Using Wild Card cartridge and purple cardstock, cut a 4-inch "a little something just for you" by selecting Phrase feature; press "<shift>" and "<Present>."

Form a 4¼ x 5½-inch side-folded card from brown cardstock. Cut a 4¼ x 4½-inch piece from white cardstock. Adhere a 4¼ x 1-inch piece of Plum Passion paper to white panel, aligning bottom edges.

Cut a 1 x 3½-inch piece from purple cardstock. Punch right edge with Scallop Edge Border Punch. Using gel pen, draw a border onto left edge of punched piece as shown. Adhere to white panel aligning top and left edges. Cut a 10-inch length from ribbon. Wrap around layered panel as shown; secure ends to back. Tie a bow with remaining ribbon; trim ends. Adhere to layered panel as shown. Insert thread through button; tie knot on back, trim ends. Adhere to bow. Adhere layered panel to card front.

Layer and adhere flowerpot pieces together as shown, using foam dots to pop up flowers. Using gel pen, draw a border around flowerpot as shown. Attach to card front using foam dots. Embellish flowers with gems.

Adhere sentiment to a 3⅜ x 4¾-inch piece of white cardstock. Adhere inside card. ●

Sources: Cricut Expression machine and cartridges from Provo Craft; white, lavender and purple cardstock and ribbon from American Crafts Inc.; remaining cardstock from Core'dinations; printed paper from Doodlebug Design Inc.; border punch from Stampin' Up!

Hop to It

Design by **Kimber McGray**

Using Paisley cartridge and Kiwi Dot paper, cut two 2-inch frogs by pressing "<Frog2>" and "<Frog2>."

Cut a 2-inch heart from Passion Fruit Dot paper by selecting Layer 2 feature; press "<Frog2>." Repeat cut.

Cut a 2-inch frog mouth from olive green cardstock by selecting Layer 1 feature; press "<Frog2>." Repeat cut.

Cut a 2-inch frog eye from white cardstock by selecting Layer 1 feature; press "<Frog2>." Repeat cut.

Using Lyrical Letters cartridge and brown cardstock, cut a 1½-inch "V" by selecting Capital feature; press "<v>." Repeat cut twice at 1-inch setting.

Cut a ½-inch "hop to it" from Buttercup Dot paper by selecting Jumbo feature; press "<h>," "<o>," "<p>," "<t>," "<o>," "<i>" and "<t>."

Cut a 2½-inch "feel better soon" sentiment from Buttercup Dot paper by selecting Loop Dee Loo feature; press "<Sorry>."

Layer and adhere frog pieces together to create two frogs.

Form a 5⅜ x 4¼-inch top-folded card from kraft paper. Adhere a 5⅜ x 3¼-inch piece of white cardstock to card front as shown.

Using foam tape, attach a frog to right side of card front. Adhere "V's" to card front as shown. Adhere "hop to it" sentiment to card front along "V's."

Wrap twine around top of card front three times; tie bow on left side, trim ends.

Adhere "feel better soon" sentiment inside card. Using foam tape, attach remaining frog inside card. ●

Sources: Cricut Expression machine and cartridges from Provo Craft; cardstock from Core'dinations; printed papers from Bo-Bunny Press.

Materials

- Cricut Expression machine
- Cartridges: Lyrical Letters (#29-0708), Paisley (#29-1591)
- Cardstock: brown, olive green, white, kraft,
- Double Dot printed papers: Buttercup Dot, Kiwi Dot, Passion Fruit Dot
- Twine
- Adhesive foam tape
- Paper adhesive

Swinging By to Say

Design by **Jennifer Buck**

Materials

- Cricut Expression machine
- Cartridges: "Just Because" Cards (#20-00097), Accent Essentials (#29-0391), Plantin SchoolBook (#29-0390), Wild Card (#29-0591)
- Cardstock: kraft, green, black, cream
- Dutch Mustard printed papers: Dry Mustard Powder, Créme Fraiche
- Brown distress dye ink pad
- Various sizes of red self-adhesive gems
- Green button
- 23 inches ⅝-inch-wide green gingham ribbon
- Twine
- Adhesive foam dots
- Paper adhesive

Project note: *Ink edges of all cut pieces brown.*

Using "Just Because" Cards cartridge and kraft cardstock, cut a 8½-inch tree base from kraft cardstock by selecting Layer 1 feature; press "<Tree>."

Cut 8½-inch tree top from green cardstock by selecting Layer 1 feature; press "<shift>" and "<Tree>."

Cut an 8½-inch swing seat from black cardstock by selecting Layer 2 feature; press "<shift>" and "<Tree>."

Using Accent Essentials cartridge and Créme Fraiche paper, cut a 4¼-inch circle by pressing "<shift>" and "<Accent1>."

Using Plantin SchoolBook cartridge and green cardstock, cut a 1-inch border of grass by pressing "<shift>" and "<city>."

Using Wild Card cartridge and black cardstock, cut "Hang in there" by selecting Phrase feature; press "<shift>" and "<Tweety>."

Form a 4⅝ x 6⅛-inch top-folded card from cream cardstock.

Cut a 4⅝ x 6⅛-inch piece from kraft cardstock and a 4½ x 6-inch piece from Dry Mustard Powder paper; ink edges. Layer and adhere pieces to card front as shown.

Adhere Créme Fraiche circle to card front allowing left edge to extend past card front's edge. Trim to align edges.

Using foam dots, attach tree top to tree base. Adhere gems to tree top as desired. Adhere swing seat to swing base. Adhere to card front as shown, allowing swing to hang free.

Adhere grass border to card front as shown, covering bottom edge of tree and allowing top of grass to hang free.

Wrap ribbon around card front as shown. Tie bow on left side, trim ends. Thread button with twine; tie knot on back; trim ends to ¾ inch long. Adhere to bow.

Adhere sentiment inside card. ●

Sources: Cricut Expression machine and cartridges from Provo Craft; printed papers from Jillibean Soup.

Get Well Soon

Design by **Lea Lawson**

Using Create A Critter cartridge and white cardstock, cut a 2-inch cloud by selecting Accessory feature; press "<Sun>."

Cut a 3-inch rainbow with heart from pink cardstock by pressing "<shift>" and "<Sun>."

Cut a 3-inch bottom rainbow layer from aqua cardstock by selecting Layers 1 feature; press "<shift>" and "<Sun>."

Cut a 3-inch middle rainbow layer from yellow cardstock by selecting Layer 2 feature; press "<shift>" and "<Sun>."

Cut a 3-inch top rainbow layer from light pink cardstock by selecting Layer 3 feature; press "<shift>" and "<Sun>."

Using Simply Sweet cartridge and white cardstock, cut a 1¼-inch "get well soon" by pressing "<getwell>."

Spread a thin layer of clear-drying glue onto cloud, yellow layer of rainbow and heart. Sprinkle glitter on top of glue. Let dry.

Form a 4½ x 4½-inch top-folded card from light pink cardstock; round bottom corners.

Cut a 4 x 4-inch piece from white cardstock; round bottom corners. Adhere to card front.

Using foam dots, attach cloud to card front as shown. Layer and adhere remaining cut pieces together as shown. Attach to card front using foam dots. Embellish with gems. ●

Sources: Cricut Expression machine and cartridges from Provo Craft; cardstock from Bazzill Basics Paper Inc.; self-adhesive gems from Doodlebug Design Inc.

Materials

- Cricut Expression machine
- Cartridges: Create A Critter (#20-00099), Simply Sweet (#29-0704)
- Cardstock: pink, light pink, white, aqua, yellow
- Large self-adhesive gems: 1 blue, 1 yellow, 1 pink
- Iridescent glitter
- Corner rounder
- Adhesive foam dots
- Clear-drying liquid glue
- Paper adhesive

thanks

Design by **Melissa Phillips**

Materials

- Cricut Expression machine
- Cartridges: Storybook (#29-0589), Opposites Attract (#29-0227)
- Cardstock: black, white
- Printed papers: Hello Luscious Tartlet, Hello Luscious Sparkling, Hello Luscious Dandy, Be Mine Love Song
- 4-inch white paper doily
- Purple self-adhesive gems: 2 small, 2 large
- 2 gray self-adhesive pearls
- White button
- 16 inches ½-inch-wide black satin ribbon
- 8 inches ½-inch-wide black seam binding
- White thread
- Paper adhesive

Using Storybook cartridge and Tartlet paper with yellow side up, cut a 4½-inch scalloped flower frame by selecting Accent/Frame feature; press "<shift>" and "<Y>." Repeat cut, this time with floral side of Tartlet paper up.

Using Opposites Attract cartridge and Dandy paper, cut a ¾-inch "thanks" by pressing "<thanks>."

Form a 5½ x 4-inch side-folded card from black cardstock.

Cut a 5¼ x 3⅞-inch piece from Sparkling paper. Adhere a 4¾ x ⅜-inch strip of Love Song paper to a 4¾ x 3⅜-inch piece of white cardstock aligning bottom edges. Center and adhere to Sparkling panel.

Cut doily in half. Adhere to layered panel, 1¼ inches above bottom edge and ½ inch from left side.

Wrap satin ribbon around layered panel as shown; tie bow, trim ends. Wrap seam binding around satin bow; tie a second bow and trim ends.

Insert white thread through button; tie knot on back, trim ends. Adhere layered panel to card front.

Trim flower from floral scalloped flower frame and adhere to yellow frame. Adhere to card front.

Adhere a 2¼ x 1-inch piece of white cardstock to yellow scalloped-flower frame. Embellish frame with gems and pearls.

Adhere "thanks" to card front as shown. ●

Sources: Cricut Expression machine and cartridges from Provo Craft; Hello Luscious printed papers from BasicGrey; Be Mine printed paper from Echo Park Paper Co.

You're the Best

Design by **Kimber McGray**

Using Lyrical Letters cartridge and brown cardstock, cut a 3-inch "You're The Best" by selecting Jumbo feature; press "<Thanks>."

Cut a 3-inch bird from Ocean Dot paper by selecting Jumbo feature; press "<shift>" and "<Thanks>." Repeat cut, adding Flip feature before cutting.

Cut a 3-inch heart from Passion Fruit Dot paper by selecting Connected feature; press "<shift>" and "<LoveU>." Repeat cut twice for a total of three cut hearts.

Cut a 2-inch heart from Passion Fruit Dot paper by selecting Connected feature; press "<shift>" and "<LoveU>."

Cut a ¾-inch "so tweet" sentiment from brown cardstock by selecting Jumbo feature; press "<s>," "<o>," "<t>," "<w>," "<e>," "<e>" and "<t>."

Form a 5½ x 4¼-inch top-folded card from kraft cardstock. Adhere a 5½ x 4¼-inch piece of Lime Wedges paper to card front as shown.

Adhere "You're the best" sentiment to right side of card front. Using foam tape, attach birds to card front as shown.

Using foam tape, attach two 3-inch hearts and one 2-inch heart to card front as shown. Embellish with pearls as shown; save one medium pearl for inside card.

Adhere "so tweet" and remaining heart inside card. Embellish heart with remaining pearl. ●

Sources: Cricut Expression machine and cartridge from Provo Craft; brown cardstock from Core'dinations; kraft cardstock and Blossom Soup printed paper from Jillibean Soup; Double Dot printed papers from Bo-Bunny Press; self-adhesive pearls from Queen & Co.

Materials

- Cricut Expression machine
- Cartridge: Lyrical Letters (#29-0708)
- Cardstock: brown, kraft
- Printed papers: Double Dot Passion Fruit Dot, Double Dot Ocean Dot, Blossom Soup Lime Wedges
- White self-adhesive pearls: 2 small, 2 medium
- Adhesive foam tape
- Paper adhesive

THANKS

Design by **Summer Fullerton**

Materials

- Cricut Expression machine
- Cartridges: Opposites Attract
- (#29-0227), Winter Woodland
- (#29-1046)
- Cardstock: kraft, yellow, light yellow, pink
- Life Is Good Floral Dress printed paper
- Small self-adhesive gems: 6 bright pink, 6 pink, 1 black
- Corner rounder
- Adhesive foam tape
- Paper adhesive

Using Opposites Attract cartridge and Floral Dress paper, cut a 2-inch "THANKS" by pressing "<shift>" and "<THANKS>."

Using Winter Woodland cartridge and kraft cardstock, cut a 2-inch branch by pressing "<Branch>."

Cut 2-inch dots for branch from pink cardstock by pressing "<shift>" and "<Branch>."

Cut a 1½-inch bird base from yellow cardstock by pressing "<Bird1>."

Cut a 1½-inch top layer of bird from light yellow cardstock by pressing "<shift>" and "<Bird1>."

Form a 6 x 4-inch top-folded card from kraft cardstock. Adhere a 6 x 4-inch piece of Floral Dress paper to card front as shown. Round corners of card using corner rounder.

Adhere "THANKS" to card front as shown.

Adhere dots to branch as shown. Embellish with gems as desired. Attach branch to card front using foam tape.

Layer and adhere bird layers together. Attach black gem to bird for eye. Attach to card front as shown with foam tape. Adhere bird's legs to branch. ●

Sources: Cricut Expression machine and cartridges from Provo Craft; cardstock from Bazzill Basics Paper Inc.; printed paper from Echo Park Paper Co.; self-adhesive gems from Doodlebug Design Inc.

Thanks for You

Design by **Kandis Smith**

Using Walk in My Garden cartridge and orange cardstock, cut a 5¼-inch tag by selecting Tag feature; press "<daisy1>." Emboss tag using Swiss Dots embossing folder.

Cut a 5¼-inch daisy from orange circles paper by selecting Tag feature; press "<shift>" and "<daisy1>."

Cut a 5¼-inch tag from light aqua cardstock by pressing "<tag>."

Cut a ¾-inch "thanks" from light aqua cardstock by pressing "<shift>" and "<abunch>."

Form a 4½ x 6-inch top-folded card from red cardstock. Adhere a 4⅛ x 5¾-inch piece of striped paper to card front. Zigzag-stitch around edges using orange thread.

Adhere embossed tag to light aqua tag. Adhere a 2 x 1⅛-inch piece of red cardstock to layered tags as shown; machine-stitch along top and bottom edges of red strip using green thread. Adhere a 2 x ½-inch green piece of cardstock to red strip as shown.

Using foam tape, adhere "thanks" to green strip.

Adhere center of orange circles flower on top of flower on layered tag, allowing flower petals to hang free.

Tie a triple bow from seam binding; scrunch bow as desired. Adhere to top of layered tag. Adhere red button to center of bow.

Insert white thread through white button; tie knot on back, trim ends. Adhere to center of flower.

Attach tag to right side of card front using foam tape. ●

Sources: Cricut Expression machine, cartridge and embossing folder from Provo Craft; cardstock from Core'dinations.

Materials

- Cricut Expression machine
- Cartridge: Walk in My Garden (#29-0223)
- Cardstock: red, orange, light aqua, green
- Printed papers: striped, orange circles
- Buttons: 1 red, 1 white
- ½-inch-wide yellow seam binding
- Thread: orange, green, white
- Swiss Dots embossing folder (#37-1604)
- Embossing machine
- Sewing machine
- Adhesive foam tape
- Paper adhesive

u r sweet cupcake

Design by **Lynn Ghahary**

Using Birthday Bash cartridge and mustard yellow cardstock, cut a 3½-inch cupcake base by pressing "<Cupcake>."

Cut a 3½-inch cupcake top from brown printed paper by pressing "<shift>" and "<Cupcake>."

Cut a 3½-inch cherry leaf from green cardstock by selecting Layer 1 feature; press "<Cupcake>."

Cut 3½-inch sprinkles from pink paper by selecting Layer 2 feature; press "<shift>" and "<Cupcake>." Repeat cut twice, once with mustard yellow cardstock and once with green cardstock.

Cut a 3½-inch "SwEeT!" sentiment base layer from pink cardstock by selecting Phrase feature; press "<Cupcake>."

Cut a 3½-inch "SwEet!" sentiment top layer from brown printed paper by selecting Phrase feature; press "<shift>" and "<Cupcake>."

Cut a 7-inch "u" from pink cardstock by selecting Layer 1 feature; press "<shift>" and "<Surprise>."

Cut a 7-inch "r" from pink cardstock by selecting Layer 2 feature; press "<Surprise>."

Form a 5½ x 4¼-inch top-folded card from green cardstock. Adhere a 5½ x 4¼-inch piece of ivory grid paper to card front.

Cut a 4 x 4¼-inch piece from green cardstock. Punch left edge of green panel with Scallop Edge Border Punch. Adhere to card front as shown.

Cut a 3 x 4¼-inch piece from pink hearts paper and a ½ x 4¼-inch piece from brown striped paper. Adhere pieces to card front as shown.

Layer and adhere cupcake pieces together as shown. Attach to card front using foam dots.

Thread button with white string; tie bow on front and trim ends. Adhere button to top of cupcake.

Layer and adhere sentiment inside card as shown. ●

Sources: Cricut Expression machine and cartridge from Provo Craft; punch from Stampin' Up!

Materials

- Cricut Expression machine
- Cartridge: Birthday Bash (#20-00585)
- Cardstock: green, mustard yellow, pink
- Coordinating printed papers: brown striped, pink hearts, brown, ivory grid
- Large pink button
- White string
- Scallop Edge Border Punch
- Adhesive foam dots
- Paper adhesive

Thank You

Design by **Lea Lawson**

Using Tie the Knot cartridge and Polka paper, cut a 5-inch scallop-edge block by selecting Invitation feature; press "<ThankYou>."

Cut a 1¾-inch heart from white cardstock by pressing "<shift>" and "<ThankYou>."

Cut a 1¾-inch thank you heart from Banner paper by pressing "<ThankYou>."

Apply glitter glue to white heart. Let dry completely.

Form a 4¼ x 5½-inch top-folded card from pink shimmer cardstock.

Trim scallop-edge block down to a 3⅝ x 3¼-inch piece as shown. Attach to card front using foam tape.

Adhere thank you heart to glitter heart. Adhere to card front.

Tie a small bow with twine; trim ends. Layer and adhere stickpin, twine bow and paper flower to upper left corner of layered heart. Attach gems to card front as shown. ●

Sources: Cricut Expression machine and cartridge from Provo Craft; pink shimmer cardstock from Bazzill Basics Paper Inc.; white cardstock from Papertrey Ink; printed papers and self-adhesive gems from Glitz Design; stickpin from Maya Road.

Materials

- Cricut Expression machine
- Cartridge: Tie the Knot (#20-00064)
- Cardstock: white, pink shimmer
- Afternoon Muse printed papers: Polka, Banner
- Aqua paper flower
- Crystal tip stickpin
- Large self-adhesive gems: 2 silver, 1 pink
- Natural twine
- Iridescent glitter glue
- Adhesive foam tape
- Paper adhesive

Sorry

Design by **Melissa Phillips**

Materials

- Cricut Expression machine
- Cartridges: Walk in My Garden (#29-0223), Doodletype (#29-0054)
- White cardstock
- Sweet Threads printed papers: Lacy Organic, Her Way, Mix and Match
- Light brown ink pad
- Aqua self-adhesive pearl
- White paper flower
- 17⅞ inches ½-inch-wide light aqua ribbon
- Cream twine
- Iridescent glitter
- Corner rounder
- Adhesive foam tape
- Clear-drying liquid glue
- Paper adhesive

Using the Walk in My Garden cartridge and Mix and Match paper, cut a 2½-inch bleeding heart stem with flowers by pressing "<bldhrt>."

Cut 2½-inch bleeding heart flowers from Lacy Organic paper by pressing "<shift>" and "<bldhrt>."

Using Doodletype cartridge and Her Way paper, cut a 1-inch "sorry" by pressing "<s>," "<o>," "<r>," "<r>" and "<y>."

Form a 5⅜ x 3¾-inch top-folded card from white cardstock; round bottom corners. Ink edges brown.

Adhere a 5⅜ x ¾-inch piece of Lacy Organic paper to card front aligning top edges.

Wrap ribbon around card front as shown; tie bow on left side, trim ends. Adhere paper flower to bow.

Spread a thin layer of clear-drying glue onto pink bleeding heart flowers. Sprinkle glitter on top of glue. Let dry.

Layer and adhere pink bleeding heart flowers to bleeding heart stem using foam tape. Adhere to card front as shown.

Tie three bows with twine; trim ends. Adhere a bow to each bleeding heart flower.

Adhere "sorry" below bleeding heart. Embellish "o" with pearl. ●

Sources: Cricut Expression machine and cartridges from Provo Craft; printed papers from BasicGrey.

Heartfelt Condolences

Design by **Sherry Wright**

Materials

- Cricut Expression machine
- Cartridges: Christmas Cards (#20-00535), Wall Décor & More (#20-00270), Wild Card (#29-0591)
- Cardstock: light blue, white, kraft
- Brown dye ink
- White button
- Brown twine
- Paper adhesive

Project note: *Ink edges of all cut pieces unless instructed otherwise.*

Using Christmas Cards cartridge and light blue cardstock, cut a 5¾-inch top-folded card by pressing "<windowcard>." ***Note:*** *Fold card to create a top-folded card with decorative edge on right side.*

Using Wall Décor & More cartridge and kraft cardstock, cut a 1-inch birds on a wire by selecting Border feature; press "<Bird>." Repeat cut using light blue cardstock.

Using Wild Card cartridge and kraft cardstock, cut a 5-inch "With Sympathy" by selecting Phrase feature; press "<Scallop>."

Adhere a 5¼ x 5¼-inch piece of white cardstock inside card; do not ink edges.

Cut two birds from light blue birds on a wire image. Adhere birds to kraft birds on a wire piece. Adhere to card front as shown.

Wrap twine around card front. Thread twine through button; tie bow on front; trim ends.

Adhere sentiment inside card as shown. ●

Sources: Cricut Expression machine and cartridges from Provo Craft; cardstock from Bazzill Basics Paper Inc.

With Sympathy

Design by **Jennifer Buck**

Materials

- Cricut Expression machine
- Cartridges: Lyrical Letters (#29-0708), Wild Card (#29-0591)
- Cardstock: cream, red, black
- Circa 1934 printed papers: Garbo, Ginger
- Dark brown ink pad
- Blue small button
- 25½ inches 1-inch-wide yellow ribbon
- Sewing machine with white thread
- Adhesive foam dot
- Paper adhesive

Project note: *Ink all edges of cut pieces.*

Using Lyrical Letters cartridge and Garbo paper, cut a 1½-inch bird by pressing "<shift>" and "<Thinking>." Repeat cut using black cardstock.

Using Wild Card cartridge and black cardstock, cut a 4½-inch "With Sympathy" by selecting Phrase feature; press "<Scallop>."

Form a 5¼ x 7¼-inch top-folded card from cream cardstock. Adhere a 5 x 7-inch piece of Ginger paper to card front. Zigzag-stitch around edge as shown.

Layer and adhere a 5 x 2¾-inch piece of red cardstock and 5 x 1½-inch piece of Ginger paper to card front as shown.

Wrap ribbon around top of card front. Tie bow on left side; trim ends.

Trim legs from black bird; adhere to Garbo bird. Attach Garbo bird to card front using foam dots. Adhere button to bird as shown.

Adhere "With Sympathy" to card front as shown. ●

Sources: Cricut Expression machine and cartridges from Provo Craft; printed papers from Cosmo Cricket.

Butterfly Sympathy

Design by **Lynn Ghahary**

Using Cake Basics cartridge and Lime Cooler paper, cut a 3¾-inch doily by pressing "<Doily1>."

Cut a 3-inch butterfly from Pink Fizz paper by pressing "<Bttrfly1>."

Cut two butterfly backgrounds from Frosted Berry paper by selecting Base Shadow Blackout feature; press "<Bttrfly1>" and "<Bttrfly1>."

Using Wild Card cartridge and Pink Fizz paper, cut a 2-inch "With Sympathy" by selecting Phrase feature; press "<Scallop>."

Form a 5 x 5-inch top-folded card from kraft cardstock. Adhere a 4¼ x 4¼-inch piece of Dandelion paper to card front as shown.

Using foam tape, attach doily to center of card front. Wrap ribbon around card front and thread through holes on doily as shown. Tie bow on left side and trim ends.

Insert pink thread through button; tie knot on back, trim ends. Adhere to bow as shown.

Adhere one butterfly background to card front as shown. Adhere remaining butterfly pieces together. Using foam tape, attach layered butterfly to card front as shown. Embellish with pearls.

Adhere sentiment inside card. ●

Sources: Cricut Expression machine and cartridges from Provo Craft; cardstock from American Crafts Inc.; printed papers from BasicGrey.

Materials

- Cricut Expression machine
- Cartridges: Cake Basics (#20-00222), Wild Card (#29-0591)
- Kraft cardstock
- Lemonade printed papers: Lime Cooler, Pink Fizz, Frosted Berry, Dandelion
- Pink button
- Pink thread
- 10 white self-adhesive pearls
- 24½ inches ¾-inch-wide gold sheer ribbon
- Adhesive foam tape
- Paper adhesive

So Sorry

Design by **Kandis Smith**

Materials

- Cricut Expression machine
- Cartridges: Walk in My Garden
- (#29-0223), Plantin SchoolBook
- (#29-0390)
- Cardstock: lavender, purple, green, kraft
- Blanche printed paper
- 2 copper brads
- Paper piercer
- Sandpaper
- Sewing machine with cream thread
- Paper adhesive

Using Walk in My Garden cartridge and green cardstock, cut a 3½-inch hyacinth border by selecting Border feature; press "<hycnth>."

Cut a 3½-inch hyacinth flower from purple cardstock by selecting Border feature; press "<shift>" and "<hycnth>." Repeat cut using lavender cardstock.

Using Plantin SchoolBook cartridge and purple cardstock, cut a ¾-inch "S" and "Y" for "So sorrY" by pressing "<shiftlock>," "<S>" and "<Y>."

Cut ½-inch "o sorr" for "So sorrY" from purple cardstock by pressing "<o>," "<s>," "<o>," "<r>" and "<r>."

Form a 7 x 3⅞-inch top-folded card from kraft cardstock. Adhere a 5½ x 3½-inch piece of printed paper to card front as shown; machine-stitch around edges.

Cut a 1¼ x 3⅞-inch piece from green cardstock. Distress piece using sandpaper. Adhere to left side of card front.

Adhere "So sorrY" to distressed green panel. Pierce a hole through card front above and below sentiment; insert brads.

Using sandpaper, distress leaves of green hyacinth border layer. Layer hyacinth pieces together. Adhere to card front as shown. ●

Sources: Cricut Expression machine and cartridges from Provo Craft; cardstock from Core'dinations; printed paper from Heart & Home Collectables Inc./Melissa Frances; brads from American Crafts Inc.

God Be With You

Design by **Kimber McGray**

Project note: *Ink all edges of cut pieces unless instructed otherwise.*

Using Pagoda cartridge and cream cardstock, cut a 5½-inch side-folded card base by selecting Card feature; press "<Flower4>." Repeat cut using olive green cardstock. ***Note:*** *Only back panel of olive green card will be used.*

Cut 5½-inch flowers from cream cardstock by pressing "<shift>" and "<Flower4>."

Using Lyrical Letters cartridge and olive green cardstock, cut a 1½-inch "God be with you" by selecting Jack Sprat feature; press "<Sorry>." Do not ink edges of sentiment yellow.

Cut a 1½-inch small flower from cream cardstock by selecting Jack Sprat feature; press "<shift>" and "<Sorry>."

Adhere olive green back panel to inside front panel of card.

Using foam dots, attach flowers to card front as shown. Embellish with pearls.

Layer and adhere sentiment and small flower inside card. ●

Sources: Cricut Expression machine and cartridges from Provo Craft; cardstock from Core'dinations; self-adhesive pearls from Queen & Co.

Materials

- Cricut Expression machine
- Cartridges: Pagoda (#29-1561), Lyrical Letters (#29-0708)
- Cardstock: cream, olive green
- Yellow chalk ink pad
- White self-adhesive pearls: 2 small, 2 large
- Adhesive foam tape
- Paper adhesive

Butterfly Thinking of You

Design by **Sherry Wright**

Materials

- Cricut Expression machine
- Cartridges: Cindy Loo (#20-00333), Sentimentals (#20-00067)
- Cardstock: light blue, cream, black
- Dye ink pads: brown, black
- Self-adhesive pearls: 2 light blue, 2 blue/gray
- Decorative stickpin
- 19 inches 1½-inch-wide light blue ribbon
- Pinking shears
- Paper adhesive

Using Cindy Loo cartridge and cream cardstock, cut a 5-inch doily by pressing "<Doily1>."

Cut a 5-inch "Thinking of You" from black cardstock by selecting Font feature; press "<Doily1>."

Using Sentimentals cartridge and light blue cardstock, cut two 1-inch butterflies by pressing "<Buttrfly>" and "<Buttrfly>." Cut off antennae.

Form a 5¼ x 5¼-inch top-folded card from light blue cardstock.

Ink edges of doily brown. Adhere to card front.

Cut a 5¼-inch length of ribbon using pinking shears. Fold in half by width and adhere to card front ⅞ inch from left edge.

Tie a bow with remaining ribbon; trim ends with pinking shears. Insert stickpin through center of bow. Adhere to card front as shown.

Referring to photo, adhere sentiment to card front.

Adhere butterflies to card front as shown, applying adhesive to bodies of butterflies only. Embellish butterflies with pearls. ●

Sources: Cricut Expression machine and cartridges from Provo Craft; cardstock from Bazzill Basics Paper Inc.

For You

Design by **Melissa Phillips**

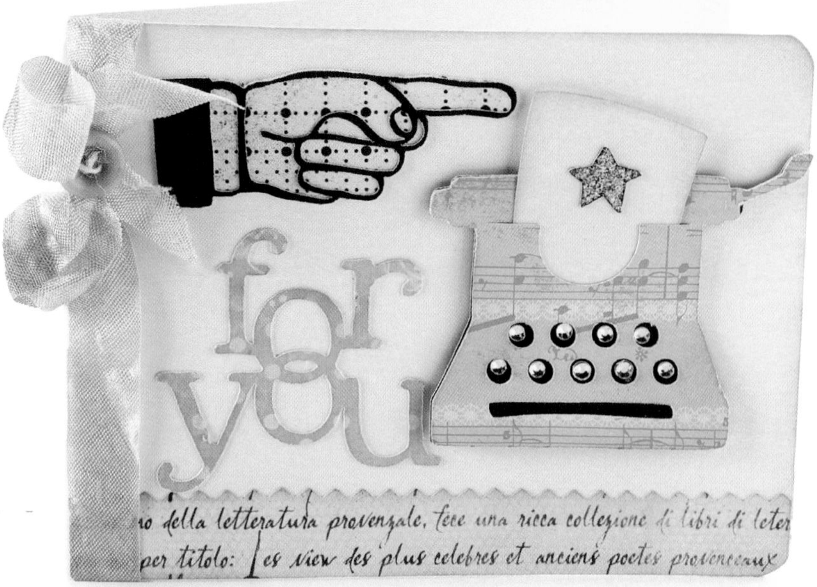

Project note: *Ink edges of cut pieces and seam binding as desired.*

Using Doodletype cartridge and pink sheet music paper, cut a 2¼-inch typewriter by pressing "<typewrtr>."

Cut a 2¼-inch typewriter background from brown printed paper by selecting Shadow Blackout feature; press "<typewrtr>."

Cut a 2¼-inch sheet of paper from cream cardstock by pressing "<shift>" and "<typewrtr>."

Cut a ½-inch star from brown printed paper by pressing "<shift>" and "<9>."

Cut a 2-inch "for you" from blue dot paper by pressing "<foryou>."

Using Graphically Speaking cartridge and Yumberry paper, cut a 1-inch hand by selecting Icon Blackout feature; press "<Image38>."

Cut a 1-inch top layer for hand from brown printed paper by selecting Icon feature; press "<Image38>."

Form a 5½ x 4¼-inch side-folded card from cream cardstock.

Cut a 5½ x ⅞-inch piece from cream script paper; trim top edge using pinking shears. Adhere to bottom of card front. Round upper and lower right corners of card using corner rounder.

Layer and adhere typewriter pieces together as shown. Insert and adhere sheet of paper piece into typewriter slot.

Apply glitter glue to star; let dry. Adhere to sheet of paper piece as shown. Embellish typewriter keys with gems. Attach assembled typewriter to right side of card front using dimensional dots.

Adhere sentiment to card front as shown. Layer and adhere hand pieces above sentiment.

Wrap seam binding around left side of card front. Tie a bow and trim ends. Insert thread through button; tie knot on back, trim ends. Adhere to bow. ●

Sources: Cricut Expression machine and cartridges from Provo Craft; Hello Luscious printed paper from BasicGrey; glitter glue from Ranger Industries Inc.

Materials

- Cricut Expression machine
- Cartridges: Doodletype (#29-0054), Graphically Speaking (#29-0590)
- Cream cardstock
- Printed papers: Hello Luscious Yumberry, pink sheet music, blue dot, cream script, brown
- Light brown ink pad
- 9 silver self-adhesive gems
- Cream button
- 15½ inches ½-inch-wide light pink seam binding
- White thread
- Corner rounder
- Pinking shears
- Gold iridescent glitter glue
- Adhesive dimensional dots
- Paper adhesive

(hugs) 2u

Design by **Summer Fullerton**

Materials

- Cricut Expression machine
- Cartridges: Doodletype (#29-0054), Plantin SchoolBook (#29-0390)
- Cardstock: brown, green, yellow
- Dutch Mustard Soup printed papers: Créme Fraiche, Dry Mustard Powder
- Yellow buttons: 1 small, 1 large
- White floss
- Adhesive foam tape
- Paper adhesive

Using Doodletype cartridge and Créme Fraiche paper, cut a 4-inch heart by pressing "<shift>"and "<8>."

Cut a 4-inch heart from yellow cardstock by selecting Shadow feature; press "<shift>" and "<8>."

Using Plantin SchoolBook cartridge and green cardstock, cut a 1½-inch "hugs 2u" by pressing "<h>," "<u>," "<g>," "<s>," "<2>" and "<u>."

Cut a 1½-inch "( )" for sentiment from green cardstock by pressing "<shift>" and "<brace>."

Form a 4 x 5-inch side-folded card from brown cardstock. Adhere a 3⅝ x 4⅝-inch piece of Dry Mustard Powder paper to card front.

Layer and adhere both hearts together. Adhere sentiment and "( )" to heart as shown. Attach to card front using foam tape.

Thread floss through large button, tie bow on front and trim ends. Thread floss through small button; tie knot on back, trim ends. Adhere buttons to card front as shown. ●

Sources: Cricut Expression machine and cartridges from Provo Craft; cardstock from Bazzill Basics Paper Inc.; printed papers from Jillibean Soup.

Wish You Were Here

Design by **Summer Fullerton**

Using Going Places cartridge and brown cardstock, cut a 2¾-inch cityscape by pressing "<cityscpe>."

Cut a 2¾-inch cityscape from kraft cardstock by selecting Shadow feature; press "<cityscpe>."

Cut a 3-inch "Wish You Were Here!" from blue cardstock by pressing "<shift>" and "<letter>."

Using Plantin SchoolBook cartridge and Leeks paper, cut a ½-inch grass border by pressing "<shiftlock>," "<city>" and "<city>."

Form a 4 x 6-inch side-folded card from white cardstock. Adhere a 4 x 6-inch piece of Corn Kernels paper to card front.

Cut small pieces from white cardstock and adhere them to back of brown cityscape, covering window holes. Embellish windows with glitter glue; let dry.

Adhere grass to bottom edge of brown cityscape. Overlap grass pieces as needed.

Layer and adhere brown cityscape to kraft cityscape using foam tape. Adhere to bottom of card front as shown.

Adhere "Wish You Were Here!" sentiment to card front as shown. Embellish with gems as desired. ●

Sources: Cricut Expression machine and cartridges from Provo Craft; cardstock from Bazzill Basics Paper Inc.; printed papers from Jillibean Soup; glitter glue from Ranger Industries Inc.

Materials

- Cricut Expression machine
- Cartridges: Going Places (#29-0291), Plantin SchoolBook (#29-0390)
- Cardstock: blue, brown, white, kraft
- Printed papers: Dutch Mustard Soup Leeks, Blossom Soup Corn Kernels
- 2 blue self-adhesive gems
- Iridescent glitter glue
- Adhesive foam tape
- Paper adhesive

i miss u

Design by **Kimber McGray**

Materials

- Cricut Expression machine
- Cartridges: Paisley (#29-1591), Lyrical Letters (#29-0708)
- Cardstock: black, gray
- Printed papers: Blossom Soup Fresh Cilantro, Double Dot Passion Fruit Dot
- White gel pen
- Scoring tool
- Adhesive foam tape
- Paper adhesive

Using Paisley cartridge and gray cardstock, cut a 5-inch cellphone card base by selecting Shadow/Word Shadow feature; press "<Cell>." Repeat cut.

Cut a 5-inch cellphone bottom layer from black cardstock by "<Cell>."

Cut a 5-inch cellphone top layer from Fresh Cilantro paper by selecting Layer 1 feature; press "<Cell>."

Cut a 5-inch cellphone screen from gray cardstock by selecting Layer 1 feature; press "<shift>" and "<Cell>."

Using Lyrical Letters cartridge and Passion Fruit Dot paper, cut a ½-inch "i miss u" by selecting Jumbo feature; press "<i>," "<m>," "<i>," "<s>," "<s>" and "<u>."

To form a side-folded card with cellphone bases, score a line vertically ¼ inch from left edge on one cellphone die cut. This will be the back panel of the card. Fold along score line; place adhesive on ¼-inch flap. Adhere remaining cellphone base for front panel of card to ¼-inch flap on back panel.

Layer and adhere cellphone pieces as shown. Using gel pen, write numbers on keypad. Adhere sentiment to cellphone screen as shown. Using foam tape, attach assembled cellphone to card front. ●

Sources: Cricut Expression machine and cartridges from Provo Craft; cardstock from Core'dinations; Blossom Soup printed paper from Jillibean Soup; Double Dot printed paper from Bo-Bunny Press.

Thinking of You

Design by **Kandis Smith**

Using Winter Woodland cartridge and gray cardstock, cut a 3-inch tag base by selecting Tag feature; press "<shift>" and "<WntrWndr>." Distress center of tag with sandpaper.

Cut a 3-inch tag top layer from gray floral paper by selecting Tag feature; press "<WntrWndr>." ***Note:*** *"Winter" will not be used for this project.*

Using Walk in My Garden cartridge and pink cardstock, cut a 1¼-inch flower by pressing "<crpsis>." Change size to 1½ inches and repeat cut.

Cut a ½-inch "of you" from white cardstock by pressing "<of you>."

Cut a ½-inch "thinking" from white cardstock by pressing "<shift>" and "<of you>."

Form a 5½ x 4¼-inch top-folded card from light pink cardstock. Adhere a 5⅛ x 3⅞-inch piece of green printed paper to card front; machine-stitch around inside edge.

Adhere "thinking of you" sentiment to gray tag as shown.

Thread two pink buttons with jute; tie knot on back of each, trim ends leaving long tails. Adhere to card front as shown.

Layer and adhere pink flowers and blue buttons to card front as shown. ●

Sources: Cricut Expression machine and cartridges from Provo Craft; cardstock from Core'dinations.

Materials

- Cricut Expression machine
- Cartridges: Winter Woodland (#29-1046), Walk in My Garden (#29-0223)
- Cardstock: pink, gray, white, light pink
- Coordinating printed papers: gray floral, green
- Various pink and blue buttons
- Natural jute
- Sandpaper
- Sewing machine with cream thread
- Adhesive foam tape
- Paper adhesive

hello

Design by **Lea Lawson**

Materials

- Cricut Expression machine
- Cartridges: Storybook (#29-0589), Straight from the Nest (#20-00190), Lyrical Letters (#29-0708), Disney© Pooh & Friends (#29-0535)
- Cardstock: cream, kraft, dark pink
- So Sophie printed papers: Clever Birds of a Feather Morning Light, Clever Family Ties Consistent Ledger, Savvy Brothers & Sisters Gracious Greenery
- 9 clear self-adhesive gems
- Iridescent glitter
- Clear-drying liquid glue
- Paper adhesive

To cut card-front panel, position a 4 x 5¼-inch piece of Birds of a Feather Morning Light paper onto lower left corner of cutting mat. Using Storybook cartridge, load paper and select Fit to Page feature. Scroll cutting blade 8 1/16 inches to the left and 6 1/16 inches down. Press "<shift>" and "<Marquee1>."

Using Straight from the Nest cartridge and kraft cardstock, cut a 4-inch tree trunk by pressing "<Tree3>."

Cut a 3½-inch outer ring and inner ring for tree from Brothers & Sisters Gracious Greenery paper by pressing "<shift>" and "<Tree3>."

Cut a 3½-inch middle ring for tree from Family Ties Consistent Ledger paper by selecting Layer/Shadow feature; press "<Tree3>."

Using Lyrical Letters cartridge and dark pink cardstock, cut a 1-inch "hello" by selecting Connected feature; press "<BstWshes>." ***Note:*** *The butterfly from this cut will not be used on this card. Save for another project.*

Using Pooh & Friends cartridge and Birds of a Feather Morning Light paper, cut a 1-inch butterfly by selecting Real Dial Size and Icon features; press "<Pooh8>." Repeat cut, adding Flip feature before cutting.

Form a 4¼ x 5½-inch top-folded card from cream cardstock. Adhere front panel to card front as shown.

Layer and adhere cut rings for tree to card front as shown. Adhere tree trunk over rings as shown.

Adhere "hello" to card front overlapping bottom of tree trunk.

Apply a thin layer of clear-drying glue to cut butterflies and sprinkle with glitter. Let dry. Adhere butterflies to card front as shown, adhering bodies of butterflies only.

Embellish tree and butterflies with gems as shown. ●

Sources: Cricut Expression machine and cartridges from Provo Craft; cream cardstock from Papertrey Ink; kraft and dark pink cardstock from Bazzill Basics Paper Inc.; printed papers from My Mind's Eye.

Love

Design by **Melissa Phillips**

Materials

- Cricut Expression machine
- Cartridges: Sweet Treats (#29-1557), Opposites Attract (#29-0227)
- Cream cardstock
- Printed papers: Be Mine Airmail Stripe, pink dot, aqua dot
- Light brown ink pad
- 2 pink small artificial flowers
- Aqua button
- White heart-tipped stickpin
- 4½ inches ⅞-inch-wide cream lace trim
- 24 inches ⅝-inch-wide pink seam binding
- White thread
- Iridescent glitter
- Adhesive dimensional dots
- Clear-drying liquid glue
- Paper adhesive

Project note: *Ink edges of pieces unless instructed otherwise.*

Using Sweet Treats cartridge and cream cardstock, cut a 5-inch circle card base by selecting Cards feature; press "<5>."

Cut a 5-inch circle from aqua dot paper by selecting Cards feature; press "<shift>" and "<5>."

Cut a 5½-inch heart from Airmail Stripe paper by selecting Layers feature; press "<shift>" and "<Cupcake5>." Repeat cut at following settings: once at 4¾ inches, once at 4½ inches and twice at 3 inches, for a total of five hearts.

Using Opposites Attract cartridge and pink dot paper, cut a 2-inch "LOVE" by pressing "<shift>" and "<love>."

Adhere aqua dot circle to card front. Adhere lace trim to card front, ⅝ inch above bottom edge.

Fold 4½-inch and 4¾-inch hearts in half; unfold. Adhere 4½-inch heart to 4¾-inch heart, applying adhesive to center of heart only, allowing sides to hang free. Adhere layered hearts to 5½-inch heart in the same manner. Adhere to card front.

Attach small hearts to either side of layered hearts as shown, using adhesive dots.

Insert thread through button; tie knot on front, trim ends. Adhere to center of layered hearts. Add flowers to card front between hearts.

Apply a thin layer of clear-drying glue to "LOVE" and sprinkle with glitter. Let dry completely. Do not ink edges light brown. Adhere to center top of card front.

Wrap seam binding around card fold. Tie a bow; trim ends. Wrap another piece of seam binding around bow; tie a second bow, trim ends. Slide stickpin through double bow, tucking sharp edge under lace trim. ●

Sources: Cricut Expression machine and cartridges from Provo Craft; Be Mine Airmail Stripe printed paper from Echo Park Paper Co.; glitter from Doodlebug Design Inc.

Wedding Congrats

Design by **Kandis Smith**

Materials

- Cricut Expression machine
- Cartridges: Wedding Solutions (#29-0544), Plantin SchoolBook (#29-0390)
- Cardstock: brown, ivory, ivory glitter
- Printed papers: blue, red
- Brown rhinestone button
- 20 inches ⅝-inch-wide ivory ribbon
- Craft knife
- Sewing machine with cream thread
- Adhesive foam tape
- Paper adhesive

Using Wedding Solutions cartridge and ivory cardstock, cut a 3¼-inch gown by pressing "<gown>."

Cut a 3¼-inch top layer gown from ivory glitter cardstock by pressing "<shift>" and "<gown>."

Using Plantin SchoolBook cartridge and red printed paper, cut a 4¼-inch circle by pressing "<circle>."

Cut a ¾-inch "congrats" from ivory cardstock by pressing "<c>," "<o>," "<n>," "<g>," "<r>," "<a>," "<t>" and "<s>."

Form a 4½ x 6⅜-inch side-folded card from brown cardstock. Cut a 4 x 6-inch piece of blue printed paper; machine-stitch along edges. Adhere to card front.

Cut a 1-inch-long slit along fold of card ¾ inch below top edge. Thread ribbon through slit and wrap ribbon around card front; tie a bow on right side of card; trim ends. Adhere button to center of bow.

Adhere red circle to card front as shown, allowing left edge to extend past edge of card. Trim edge even.

Adhere sentiment along right edge of circle as shown. Layer and adhere gown pieces; attach to card front using foam tape. ●

Sources: Cricut Expression machine and cartridges from Provo Craft; rhinestone button from Webster's Pages.

Baby Boy

Design by **Jennifer Buck**

Project note: *Ink edges of all cut pieces.*

Using "Just Because" Cards cartridge and kraft cardstock, cut a 4½-inch sailboat base by selecting Layer 1 feature; press "<Boat>."

Cut a 4-inch sailboat body from Cornmeal paper by selecting Layer 1 feature; press "<shift>" and "<Boat>."

Cut 4-inch sailboat sails from Fresh Cilantro paper by selecting Layer 2 feature; press "<Boat>."

Cut a 4-inch sailboat flag from red cardstock by selecting Layer 2 feature; press "<shift>" and "<Boat>."

Form a 5½ x 6½-inch top-folded card from white natural cardstock. Adhere a 5½ x 6½-inch piece of Wholegrain Mustard paper to card front. Center and adhere a 3⅞ x 6½-inch piece of Cornmeal paper to card front.

Cut a 4¾ x 5-inch piece from kraft cardstock; round bottom corners using corner rounder. Adhere to card front. Wrap ribbon around top of card front; tie bow on left side, trim ends.

Layer and adhere sailboat pieces together. Attach to card front using foam tape. ●

Sources: Cricut Expression machine and cartridge from Provo Craft; printed papers from Jillibean Soup.

Materials

- Cricut Expression machine
- Cartridge: "Just Because" Cards (#20-00097)
- Cardstock: kraft, red, white natural
- Printed papers: Blossom Soup Fresh Cilantro, Blossom Soup Cornmeal, Dutch Mustard Wholegrain Mustard
- Brown ink pad
- 27 inches ⅝-inch-wide green ribbon
- Corner rounder
- Adhesive foam tape
- Paper adhesive

It's a Girl

Design by **Kimber McGray**

Materials

- Cricut Expression machine
- Cartridges: "Just Because" Cards (#20-00097), Wild Card (#29-0591)
- Cardstock: pink, white
- Printed papers: Pasta Fagioli Meatballs, Egg Drop Soup White Pepper
- Pink craft felt
- White gel pen
- 11 inches ½-inch-wide white silk ribbon
- Adhesive foam tape
- Paper adhesive

Using "Just Because" Cards cartridge and White Pepper paper, cut a 5½-inch card base by pressing "<Apple>." Repeat cut using white cardstock.

Cut a 5½-inch-long scalloped edge from Meatballs paper by pressing "<shift>" and "<Apple>."

Using Wild Card cartridge and craft felt, cut a 5½-inch safety pin by selecting Frame feature; press "<shift>" and "<SaftyPin>."

Cut a 5½-inch "It's a Girl" sentiment from white cardstock by selecting Phrase feature; press "<SaftyPin>."

Adhere white card inside White Pepper card as shown.

Adhere Meatballs scalloped edge piece to bottom edge of card front, aligning scalloped edges.

Adhere a 5½ x 1¼-inch piece of pink cardstock to card front as shown. Using gel pen, draw a dashed line along bottom edge.

Wrap silk ribbon around felt safety pin as shown; tie bow and trim ends. Attach to card front using foam tape. Adhere sentiment to card front as shown. ●

Sources: Cricut Expression machine and cartridges from Provo Craft; cardstock from Core'dinations; printed papers from Jillibean Soup.

You Did It!

Design by **Kelly Goree**

Materials

- Cricut Expression machine
- Cartridges: Simply Sweet (#29-0704), Beyond Birthdays
- (#29-0024)
- Cardstock: kraft, cream, orange
- Rocket Age printed papers: Incoming Transmission, Black Hole, Space Station, Captain's Log
- Blue dye ink pad
- White opaque spray ink
- Pens: black fine-tip, white gel
- Blue/white baker's twine
- Adhesive foam tape
- Paper adhesive

Using Simply Sweet cartridge and Incoming Transmission paper, cut a 3-inch star by pressing "<shift>" and "<congrats>." Repeat cut. ***Note:*** *You will be using center of cut star for this project. Save star outline for another project.*

Cut a 4-inch star from Black Hole paper by pressing "<shift>" and "<congrats>."

Using Beyond Birthdays cartridge and Space Station paper, cut a 2-inch "you did it" by pressing "<udidit>."

Cut a 2-inch "you did it" shadow from orange cardstock by selecting Shadow feature; press "<udidit>."

Cut a 2-inch star from cream cardstock by pressing "<shift>" and "<udidit>." Repeat twice for a total of three stars.

Form a 7 x 5-inch top-folded card from kraft cardstock. Spray card front with opaque spray ink; let dry completely. Ink edges of card front blue.

Adhere a 6¾ x 4¾-inch piece of Captain's Log paper to card front adding dashed lines around edge with a black fine-tip pen.

Adhere Incoming Transmission stars and Black Hole star to card front as shown, allowing stars to extend past edges of card front. Trim edges even. Wrap baker's twine around card front three times; tie bow on right side, trim ends.

Layer and adhere sentiment and sentiment shadow together. Referring to photo for placement, draw dashed lines across sentiment with white gel pen.

In the same manner as before, draw dashed border around cream stars. Adhere one cream star to sentiment.

Using foam tape, attach layered sentiment to card front. Adhere remaining cream stars to card front as shown, using foam tape on one. ●

Sources: Cricut Expression machine and cartridges from Provo Craft; cardstock from Bazzill Basics Paper Inc.; printed papers from October Afternoon; opaque spray ink from Studio Calico.

New Home

Design by **Lynn Ghahary**

Materials

- Cricut Expression machine
- Cartridges: Plantin SchoolBook (#29-0390), April Showers (#20-00901), Simply Sweet (#29-0704)
- Cardstock: kraft, white, red, green, yellow, brown
- Printed papers: blue, red
- Self-adhesive dimensional dots: 1 yellow, 1 red
- Yellow button
- Embroidery floss: green, yellow
- Large sewing needle
- Scalloped Edge Border Punch
- Adhesive foam tape
- Paper adhesive

Using Plantin SchoolBook cartridge and green cardstock, cut 1-inch grass by pressing "<shift>" and "<city>."

Using April Showers cartridge and blue printed paper, cut a 1½-inch cloud by pressing "<Cloud>."

Cut a 3¼-inch house base from brown cardstock by pressing "<House2>."

Cut a 3¼-inch house top layer from red printed paper by pressing "<House2Lyr>."

Cut one ½-inch flower from yellow cardstock by pressing "<Flower1>." Repeat cut.

Cut one ¾-inch flower from yellow cardstock by pressing "<Flower>."

Using Simply Sweet cartridge and red printed paper, cut a 2-inch "CoNgRats" sentiment by selecting Blocked feature; press "<congrats>."

Cut a 2-inch sentiment background block from brown cardstock by selecting Blockout feature; press "<congrats>." Repeat cut using white cardstock.

Form a 5 x 5-inch top-folded card from kraft cardstock. Adhere a 4½ x 4½-inch piece of white cardstock to card front.

Cut a ½ x 4-inch piece from red cardstock. Punch left edge with Scalloped Edge Border Punch. Adhere to card front as shown, allowing scalloped edge to extend past left side of card front. Adhere grass and cloud to card front as shown.

Layer and adhere house pieces together. Attach to card front using foam tape. Add doorknob by attaching yellow dimensional dot to door. Adhere flowers to card front as shown, using foam tape as desired to pop up flowers. Place red dimensional dot on center of large flower.

Thread button with yellow floss; tie knot on back, trim ends. Adhere to cloud as shown.

Using needle and green floss, hand-stitch two X's through card front along top right edge of white panel.

Adhere sentiment block to white background block. Adhere brown background block and sentiment block inside card as shown. Using needle and green floss, hand-stitch X's inside card as desired. ●

Sources: Cricut Expression machine and cartridges from Provo Craft; cardstock from American Crafts Inc.; self-adhesive Candy Dots from Pebbles Inc.; punch from Stampin' Up!

Baby Congrats!

Design by **Summer Fullerton**

Using Going Places cartridge and brown cardstock, cut a 4-inch card base by selecting Shadow feature; press "<card>." Fold to create a side-folded card.

Cut a 3¾-inch pregnant image panel from Complete Set paper by selecting Sign feature; press "<momtobe>."

Cut a 1½-inch tag from kraft cardstock by pressing "<shift>" and "<rolirbag>."

Using Accent Essentials cartridge and green cardstock, cut ½-inch flowers by pressing "<Accent24>." Repeat twice for a total of three flowers.

Adhere a 3 x 3¾-inch piece of red cardstock to back of pregnant image panel. Referring to photo, pierce three holes through layered panel; slide brads through flowers and then through holes. Adhere panel to card front.

Use a fine-tip pen to hand-print "CONGRATS!" onto tag. ***Note:*** *Instead of hand-printing, use alphabet stamps or rub-on transfers to create word on tag.* Thread twine through hole on tag. Wrap twine around card fold; tie bow and trim ends. ●

Sources: Cricut Expression machine and cartridges from Provo Craft; cardstock from Bazzill Basics Paper Inc.; printed paper from October Afternoon.

Materials

- Cricut Expression machine
- Cartridges: Going Places (#29-0291), Accent Essentials (#29-0391)
- Cardstock: red, kraft, brown, green
- The Thrift Shop Complete Set printed paper
- Black fine-tip pen
- 3 green brads
- White twine
- Paper piercer
- Paper adhesive

Gentle Baby

Design by **Lea Lawson**

Materials

- Cricut Expression machine
- Cartridges: Graphically Speaking (#29-0590), Plantin SchoolBook (#29-0390)
- Cardstock: light yellow, aqua, cream
- Lush Blue Large Polka Dot printed paper
- 3 yellow self-adhesive pearls
- Paper flowers: 1 yellow, 1 aqua
- 12 inches ½-inch-wide cream ribbon
- Iridescent glitter
- Clear-drying liquid glue
- Paper adhesive

Using Graphically Speaking cartridge and cream cardstock, cut a 2½-inch gentle block by selecting Word feature; press "<Image08>."

Cut a 1¾-inch moon from aqua cardstock by selecting Word feature; press "<shift>" and "<Image05>."

Using Plantin SchoolBook cartridge and light yellow cardstock; cut a ¾-inch star by selecting Roly Poly feature; press "<star>." Repeat twice for a total of three stars.

Cut a 1-inch "baby" sentiment from aqua cardstock by selecting Tall Ball feature and pressing "<b>," "<a>," "<b>" and "<y>."

Form a 5½ x 4¼-inch top-folded card from light yellow cardstock. Adhere a 5¼ x 4-inch piece of printed paper to card front.

Adhere a 4⅛ x 2-inch piece of light yellow cardstock to back of gentle block, trimming edges even as needed. Adhere to center top of card front. Adhere "baby" to card front as shown.

Apply a thin layer of clear-drying glue onto stars; sprinkle with glitter. Let dry. Referring to photo, adhere stars to card front. Embellish stars with yellow pearls.

Adhere moon to card front to the left of stars.

Tie a bow with ribbon; trim ends and adhere to upper left corner of card front. Adhere flowers to bow. ●

Sources: Cricut Expression machine and cartridge from Provo Craft; yellow and aqua cardstock from Bazzill Basics Paper Inc.; cream cardstock from Papertrey Ink; printed paper from My Mind's Eye; pearls from Kaisercraft; paper flowers from Michaels Stores Inc.; glitter from Doodlebug Design Inc.

Happy 50th Anniversary

Design by **Kimber McGray**

Using Jubilee cartridge and Buttercup Dot paper, cut a 3½-inch champagne glass by selecting Stilts feature; press "<shift>" and "<Enjoy>." Repeat cut.

Cut a 4-inch "50" from black cardstock by selecting Runt feature; press "<5>" and "<0>."

Cut a 1-inch "happy anniversary" and "th" from black cardstock by selecting Runt feature; press "<h>," "<a>," "<p>," "<p>," "<y>," "<a>," "<n>," "<n>," "<i>," "<v>," "<e>," "<r>," "<s>," "<a>," "<r>," "<y>," "<t>" and "<h>."

Form a 4¼ x 5½-inch top-folded card from Buttercup Dot paper. Cut a 3¾ x 5⅛-inch piece from white cardstock. Trim corners as shown; attach to card front using foam tape.

With ribbon, tie a bow around one champagne glass; trim ends. Adhere champagne glasses to card front as shown, using foam tape to attach glass with bow.

Use foam tape to attach "50" to card front. Adhere "happy anniversary" and "th" to card front as shown. Embellish champagne glasses with pearls. ●

Sources: Cricut Expression machine and cartridge from Provo Craft; cardstock from Core'dinations; printed paper from Bo-Bunny Press; self-adhesive pearls from Queen & Co.; ribbon from Creative Impressions Inc.

Materials

- Cricut Expression machine
- Cartridge: Jubilee (#29-0706)
- Cardstock: black, white
- Double Dot Buttercup Dot printed paper
- Various sizes of white self-adhesive pearls
- 10 inches ½-inch-wide white silk ribbon
- Adhesive foam tape
- Paper adhesive

Congrats

Design by **Sherry Wright**

Using Country Life cartridge and Refreshing paper, cut a 1¼-inch banner by selecting Banner feature; press "<shift>" and "<papa>." Repeat cut. In the same manner, cut two banners from Celebrate Life paper, Tea Time paper and Fresh Air paper for a total of eight banners.

Using Wild Card cartridge and Refreshing paper, cut a 5½-inch "Congrats" by selecting Phrase feature; press "<shift>" and "<#1>."

Form a 4 x 6¼-inch side-folded card from red cardstock.

Cut a 3¾ x 5¾-inch piece from kraft cardstock. Using Swiss Dots embossing folder, emboss kraft panel. Adhere to card front.

Ink edges of banners. Adhere to card front as shown. Adhere a piece of twine along top edges of banners. Tie four small bows using twine; trim ends. Adhere to card front as shown. Referring to photo, adhere "Congrats" to card front. ●

Sources: Cricut Expression machine, cartridges and embossing folder from Provo Craft; cardstock from Bazzill Basics Paper Inc.; printed papers from Webster's Pages.

Materials

- Cricut Expression machine
- Cartridges: Country Life (#20-00371), Wild Card (#29-0591)
- Cardstock: kraft, red
- Garden Gala printed papers: Celebrate Life, Tea Time, Fresh Air, Refreshing
- Brown ink pad
- Brown twine
- Swiss Dots embossing folder (#37-1604)
- Embossing machine
- Paper adhesive

Contributors

Jennifer Buck
http://thebuckstampshere.blogspot.com/
Baby Boy, 40
Birthday Cupcake, 8
Milk It, 13
Swinging By to Say, 17
With Sympathy, 27

Summer Fullerton
http://summerfullerton.typepad.com/
Baby Congrats!, 44
Happy Birthday, 6
(hugs) 2u, 33
THANKS, 21
Wish You Were Here, 34

Lynn Ghahary
http://lynnghahary.blogspot.com/
Butterfly Sympathy, 28
Hang In There, 12
Happy Birthday Dad, 9
New Home, 43
Just for You, 15
u r sweet cupcake, 23

Kelly Goree
http://kellygoree.blogspot.com/
To Perk You Up, 14
You Did It!, 42

Lea Lawson
http://leascupcakesandsunshine.blogspot.com/
Gentle Baby, 45
Get Well Soon, 18
hello, 37
Thank You, 24

Kimber McGray
http://kimbermcgray.blogspot.com/
It's a Girl, 41
God Be With You, 30
Happy 50th Anniversary, 46
Hop to It, 16
i miss u, 35
Shop Til You Drop, 3
You're the Best, 20

Melissa Phillips
http://lilybeanpaperie.typepad.com/lilybeans_paperie/
Enjoy, 4
For You, 32
Ice Cream Cone Card, 5
Love, 38
Sorry, 25
thanks, 19

Kandis Smith
http://www.mycreativetreasury.blogspot.com/
Feel Better, 11
Happy Day, 7
So Sorry, 30
Thanks for You, 22
Thinking of You, 36
Wedding Congrats, 39

Sherry Wright
http://sherrywright.typepad.com/
Butterfly Thinking of You, 31
Congrats, 47
Happy B-day, 10
Heartfelt Condolences, 26

Buyer's Guide

American Crafts Inc.
(801) 226-0747
www.americancrafts.com

BasicGrey
(801) 544-1116
www.basicgrey.com

Bazzill Basics Paper Inc.
(800) 560-1610
www.bazzillbasics.com

Bo-Bunny Press
(801) 771-4010
www.bobunny.com

Core'dinations
www.coredinations.com

Cosmo Cricket
(800) 852-8810
www.cosmocricket.com

Creative Impressions Inc.
(719) 596-4860
www.creativeimpressions.com

Doodlebug Design Inc.
(801) 952-0555
www.doodlebugdesign.homestead.com

Echo Park Paper Co.
(800) 701-1115
www.echoparkpaper.com

EK Success
www.eksuccess.com

Glitz Design
(866) 356-6131
www.glitzitnow.com

Graphic 45
(866) 573-4806
www.g45papers.com

Heart & Home Collectables Inc./Melissa Frances
(484) 248-6080
www.heartandhome.com

Jillibean Soup
(888) 212-1177
www.jillibean-soup.com

Kaisercraft
(888) 684-7147
www.kaisercraft.net

Making Memories
www.makingmemories.com

Maya Road
(877) 427-7764
www.mayaroad.com

Michaels Stores Inc.
(800) MICHAELS (642-4235)
www.michaels.com

My Mind's Eye
(800) 665-5116
www.mymindseye.com

October Afternoon
(866) 513-5553
www.octoberafternoon.com

Papertrey Ink
www.papertreyink.com

Pebbles Inc.
(800) 438-8153
www.pebblesinc.com

Provo Craft
(800) 937-7686
www.provocraft.com

Queen & Co.
www.queenandco.com

Ranger Industries Inc.
(732) 389-3535
www.rangerink.com

Stampin' Up!
(800) STAMP UP (782-6787)
www.stampinup.com

Studio Calico
www.studiocalico.com

Webster's Pages
(800) 543-6104
www.websterspages.com

Zva Creative
(801) 243-9281
www.zvacreative.com

The Buyer's Guide listings are provided as a service to our readers and should not be considered an endorsement from this publication.